❖

HOUSE OF LIGHT

HOUSE OF LIGHT

MARY OLIVER

BEACON PRESS   BOSTON

Beacon Press
25 Beacon Street
Boston, Massachusetts 02108-2892
www.beacon.org

Beacon Press books
are published under the auspices of
the Unitarian Universalist Association of Congregations.

26 25 24 23 36 35 34 33

Text design by Dede Cummings

My thanks to the editors of the following magazines, in which some of these poems
previously appeared:
Amicus (Spring, The Pipefish, The Swan, Five A.M. in the Pinewoods); *Antaeus* (Nature);
The Atlantic (Lilies, Writing Poems, Moccasin Flowers, The Loon on Oak-Head Pond);
Country Journal (The Deer, The Gift, Wings, The Notebook, Herons in Winter in the Frozen
Marsh, How Turtles Come to Spend the Winter in the Aquarium . . . , Finches, Turtle);
Harvard Magazine (Some Questions You Might Ask); *Kenyon Review* (Fish Bones,
Indonesia, The Terns); *Ohio Review* (Crows); *Partisan Review* (Everything); *Ploughshares*
(Maybe, Little Owl Who Lives in the Orchard); *Poetry* (The Hermit Crab, The Kingfisher,
Singapore, Death at a Great Distance, Snake, What Is It?); *Sycamore Review* (The
Kookaburras); *Virginia Quarterly Review* (The Buddha's Last Instruction, The Lilies Break
Open Over the Dark Water); *Western Humanities Review* (Praise, "Ich bin der Welt abhanden
gekommen"); *Wigwag* (The Summer Day, Some Herons); *Wilderness* (The Ponds). White
Owl Flies Into and Out of the Field originally appeared in *The New Yorker*.

This book is printed on acid-free paper that meets the uncoated paper ANSI/NISO
specifications for permanence as revised in 1992.

Library of Congress Cataloging-in-Publication Data

Oliver, Mary
    House of light / Mary Oliver.
        p.   cm.
    ISBN 978-0-8070-6811-3 (pbk.)
    I. Title.
PS3565.L5H68.   1990
811'.54—dc20   89-46059

For
Molly Malone Cook

Contents

❖

HOUSE OF LIGHT

SOME QUESTIONS YOU MIGHT ASK

Is the soul solid, like iron?
Or is it tender and breakable, like
the wings of a moth in the beak of the owl?
Who has it, and who doesn't?
I keep looking around me.
The face of the moose is as sad
as the face of Jesus.
The swan opens her white wings slowly.
In the fall, the black bear carries leaves into the darkness.
One question leads to another.
Does it have a shape? Like an iceberg?
Like the eye of a hummingbird?
Does it have one lung, like the snake and the scallop?
Why should I have it, and not the anteater
who loves her children?
Why should I have it, and not the camel?
Come to think of it, what about the maple trees?
What about the blue iris?
What about all the little stones, sitting alone in the moonlight?
What about roses, and lemons, and their shining leaves!
What about the grass!

Moccasin Flowers

All my life,
   so far,
      I have loved
         more than one thing,

including the mossy hooves
   of dreams, including
      the spongy litter
         under the tall trees.

In spring
   the moccasin flowers
      reach for the crackling
         lick of the sun

and burn down. Sometimes,
   in the shadows,
      I see the hazy eyes,
         the lamb-lips

of oblivion,
   its deep drowse,
      and I can imagine a new nothing
         in the universe,

the matted leaves splitting
   open, revealing
      the black planks
         of the stairs.

But all my life—so far—
   I have loved best
      how the flowers rise
      and open, how

the pink lungs of their bodies
   enter the fire of the world
      and stand there shining
      and willing—the one

thing they can do before
   they shuffle forward
      into the floor of darkness, they
      become the trees.

THE BUDDHA'S LAST INSTRUCTION

"Make of yourself a light,"
said the Buddha,
before he died.
I think of this every morning
as the east begins
to tear off its many clouds
of darkness, to send up the first
signal—a white fan
streaked with pink and violet,
even green.
An old man, he lay down
between two sala trees,
and he might have said anything,
knowing it was his final hour.
The light burns upward,
it thickens and settles over the fields.
Around him, the villagers gathered
and stretched forward to listen.
Even before the sun itself
hangs, disattached, in the blue air,
I am touched everywhere
by its ocean of yellow waves.
No doubt he thought of everything
that had happened in his difficult life.
And then I feel the sun itself
as it blazes over the hills,
like a million flowers on fire—
clearly I'm not needed,

yet I feel myself turning
into something of inexplicable value.
Slowly, beneath the branches,
he raised his head.
He looked into the faces of that frightened crowd.

Spring

Somewhere
  a black bear
    has just risen from sleep
      and is staring

down the mountain.
  All night
    in the brisk and shallow restlessness
      of early spring

I think of her,
  her four black fists
    flicking the gravel,
      her tongue

like a red fire
  touching the grass,
    the cold water.
      There is only one question:

how to love this world.
  I think of her
    rising
      like a black and leafy ledge

to sharpen her claws against
  the silence
    of the trees.
      Whatever else

my life is
   with its poems
      and its music
         and its glass cities,

it is also this dazzling darkness
   coming
      down the mountain,
         breathing and tasting;

all day I think of her—
   her white teeth,
      her wordlessness,
         her perfect love.

SINGAPORE

In Singapore, in the airport,
a darkness was ripped from my eyes.
In the women's restroom, one compartment stood open.
A woman knelt there, washing something
   in the white bowl.

Disgust argued in my stomach
and I felt, in my pocket, for my ticket.

A poem should always have birds in it.
Kingfishers, say, with their bold eyes and gaudy wings.
Rivers are pleasant, and of course trees.
A waterfall, or if that's not possible, a fountain
   rising and falling.
A person wants to stand in a happy place, in a poem.

When the woman turned I could not answer her face.
Her beauty and her embarrassment struggled together, and
   neither could win.
She smiled and I smiled. What kind of nonsense is this?
Everybody needs a job.

Yes, a person wants to stand in a happy place, in a poem.
But first we must watch her as she stares down at her labor,
   which is dull enough.
She is washing the tops of the airport ashtrays, as big as
   hubcaps, with a blue rag.
Her small hands turn the metal, scrubbing and rinsing.
She does not work slowly, nor quickly, but like a river.
Her dark hair is like the wing of a bird.

I don't doubt for a moment that she loves her life.
And I want her to rise up from the crust and the slop
    and fly down to the river.
This probably won't happen.
But maybe it will.
If the world were only pain and logic, who would want it?

Of course, it isn't.
Neither do I mean anything miraculous, but only
the light that can shine out of a life. I mean
the way she unfolded and refolded the blue cloth,
the way her smile was only for my sake; I mean
the way this poem is filled with trees, and birds.

The Hermit Crab

Once I looked inside
    the darkness
        of a shell folded like a pastry,
            and there was a fancy face—

or almost a face—
    it turned away
        and frisked up its brawny forearms
            so quickly

against the light
    and my looking in
        I scarcely had time to see it,
            gleaming

under the pure white roof
    of old calcium.
        When I set it down, it hurried
            along the tideline

of the sea,
    which was slashing along as usual,
        shouting and hissing
            toward the future,

turning its back
    with every tide on the past,
        leaving the shore littered
            every morning

with more ornaments of death—
   what a pearly rubble
      from which to choose a house
        like a white flower—

and what a rebellion
   to leap into it
     and hold on,
        connecting everything,

the past to the future—
   which is of course the miracle—
      which is the only argument there is
        against the sea.

LILIES

I have been thinking
about living
like the lilies
that blow in the fields.

They rise and fall
in the wedge of the wind,
and have no shelter
from the tongues of the cattle,

and have no closets or cupboards,
and have no legs.
Still I would like to be
as wonderful

as that old idea.
But if I were a lily
I think I would wait all day
for the green face

of the hummingbird
to touch me.
What I mean is,
could I forget myself

even in those feathery fields?
When van Gogh
preached to the poor
of course he wanted to save someone—

most of all himself.
He wasn't a lily,
and wandering through the bright fields
only gave him more ideas

it would take his life to solve.
I think I will always be lonely
in this world, where the cattle
graze like a black and white river—

where the ravishing lilies
melt, without protest, on their tongues—
where the hummingbird, whenever there is a fuss,
just rises and floats away.

WINGS

I saw the heron
  poise
    like a branch of white petals
     in the swamp,

in the mud that lies
  like a glaze,
    in the water
     that swirls its pale panels

of reflected clouds;
  I saw the heron shaking
    its damp wings—
     and then I felt

an explosion—
  a pain—
    also a happiness
     I can hardly mention

as I slid free—
  as I saw the world
    through those yellow eyes—
     as I stood like that, rippling,

under the mottled sky
  of the evening
    that was beginning to throw
     its dense shadows.

No! said my heart, and drew back.
  But my bones knew something wonderful
    about the darkness—
      and they thrashed in their cords,

they fought, they wanted
  to lie down in that silky mash
    of the swamp, the sooner
      to fly.

The Swan

Across the wide waters
   something comes
     floating—a slim
      and delicate

ship, filled
   with white flowers—
     and it moves
      on its miraculous muscles

as though time didn't exist,
   as though bringing such gifts
     to the dry shore
      was a happiness

almost beyond bearing.
   And now it turns its dark eyes,
     it rearranges
      the clouds of its wings,

it trails
   an elaborate webbed foot,
     the color of charcoal.
      Soon it will be here.

Oh, what shall I do
   when that poppy-colored beak
     rests in my hand?
      Said Mrs. Blake of the poet:

I miss my husband's company—
   he is so often
      in paradise.
         Of course! the path to heaven

doesn't lie down in flat miles.
   It's in the imagination
      with which you perceive
         this world,

and the gestures
   with which you honor it.
      Oh, what will I do, what will I say, when those
         white wings
         touch the shore?

THE KINGFISHER

The kingfisher rises out of the black wave
like a blue flower, in his beak
he carries a silver leaf. I think this is
the prettiest world—so long as you don't mind
a little dying, how could there be a day in your whole life
that doesn't have its splash of happiness?
There are more fish than there are leaves
on a thousand trees, and anyway the kingfisher
wasn't born to think about it, or anything else.
When the wave snaps shut over his blue head, the water
remains water—hunger is the only story
he has ever heard in his life that he could believe.
I don't say he's right. Neither
do I say he's wrong. Religiously he swallows the silver leaf
with its broken red river, and with a rough and easy cry
I couldn't rouse out of my thoughtful body
if my life depended on it, he swings back
over the bright sea to do the same thing, to do it
(as I long to do something, anything) perfectly.

INDONESIA

On the curving, dusty roads
we drove through the plantations
where the pickers balanced on the hot hillsides—
then we climbed toward the green trees,
toward the white scarves of the clouds,
to the inn that is never closed
in this island of fairest weather.
The sun hung like a stone,
time dripped away like a steaming river
and from somewhere a dry tongue lashed out
its single motto: now and forever.
And the pickers balanced on the hot hillsides
like gray and blue blossoms,
wrapped in their heavy layers of clothes
against the whips of the branches
in that world of leaves no poor man,
with a brown face and an empty sack,
has ever picked his way out of.
At the inn we stepped from the car
to the garden, where tea
was brought to us scalding in white cups from the fire.
Don't ask if it was the fire of honey
or the fire of death, don't ask
if we were determined to live, at last,
with merciful hearts. We sat
among the unforgettable flowers.
We let the white cups cool before
we raised them to our lips.

"ICH BIN DER WELT ABHANDEN GEKOMMEN"

Today is
  Gustav Mahler's
    birthday, and
      as usual I went out

early into the sea-green
  morning where the birds
    were singing,
      all over but mostly

at the scalloped edges
  of the ponds
    and in the branches of the trees,
      which flared out and down,

like the clothes of our spirits
  patiently waiting.
    For hours I wandered
      over the fields

and the only thing that kept me company
  was a song,
    it glided along
      with my delicious dark happiness,

my heavy,
  bristling and aching delight
    at the world
      which has been like this

forever and forever—
   the leaves,
      the birds, the ponds,
         the loneliness,

and, sometimes,
   from a lifetime ago
      and another country
         such a willing and lilting companion—

a song
   made so obviously for me.
      At what unknowable cost.
      And by a stranger.

Turtle

Now I see it—
it nudges with its bulldog head
the slippery stems of the lilies, making them tremble;
and now it noses along in the wake of the little brown teal

who is leading her soft children
from one side of the pond to the other; she keeps
close to the edge
and they follow closely, the good children—

the tender children,
the sweet children, dangling their pretty feet
into the darkness.
And now will come—I can count on it—the murky splash,

the certain victory
of that pink and gassy mouth, and the frantic
circling of the hen while the rest of the chicks
flare away over the water and into the reeds, and my heart

will be most mournful
on their account. But, listen,
what's important?
Nothing's important

except that the great and cruel mystery of the world,
of which this is a part,
not be denied. Once,
I happened to see, on a city street, in summer,

a dusty, fouled turtle plodding along—
a snapper—
broken out I suppose from some backyard cage—
and I knew what I had to do—

I looked it right in the eyes, and I caught it—
I put it, like a small mountain range,
into a knapsack, and I took it out
of the city, and I let it

down into the dark pond, into
the cool water,
and the light of the lilies,
to live.

The Deer

You never know.
The body of night opens
like a river, it drifts upward like white smoke,

like so many wrappings of mist.
And on the hillside two deer are walking along
just as though this wasn't

the owned, tilled earth of today
but the past.
I did not see them the next day, or the next,

but in my mind's eye—
there they are, in the long grass,
like two sisters.

This is the earnest work. Each of us is given
only so many mornings to do it—
to look around and love

the oily fur of our lives,
the hoof and the grass-stained muzzle.
Days I don't do this

I feel the terror of idleness,
like a red thirst.
Death isn't just an idea.

When we die the body breaks open
like a river;
the old body goes on, climbing the hill.

The Loon on Oak-Head Pond

cries for three days, in the gray mist.
cries for the north it hopes it can find.

plunges, and comes up with a slapping pickerel.
blinks its red eye.

cries again.

you come every afternoon, and wait to hear it.
you sit a long time, quiet, under the thick pines,
in the silence that follows.

as though it were your own twilight.
as though it were your own vanishing song.

WHAT IS IT?

Who can say,
is it a snowy egret
or a white flower
standing

at the glossy edge
of the lily-
and frog-filled pond?
Hours ago the orange sun

opened the cups of the lilies
and the leopard frogs
began kicking
their long muscles,

breast-stroking
like little green dwarves
under the roof of the rich,
iron-colored water.

Now the soft
eggs of the salamander
in their wrappings of jelly
begin to shiver.

They're tired of sleep.
They have a new idea.
They want to swim away
into the world.

Who could stop them?
Who could tell them
to go cautiously, to flow slowly
under the lily pads?

Off they go,
hundreds of them,
like the black
fingerprints of the rain.

The frogs freeze
into perfect five-fingered
shadows, but suddenly the flower
has fire-colored eyes

and one of the shadows vanishes.
Clearly, now, the flower is a bird.
It lifts its head,
it lifts the hinges

of its snowy wings,
tossing a moment of light
in every direction,
like a chandelier,

and then once more is still.
The salamanders,
like tiny birds, locked into formation,
fly down into the endless mysteries

of the transforming water,
and how could anyone believe
that anything in this world
is only what it appears to be—

that anything is ever final—
that anything, in spite of its absence,
ever dies
a perfect death?

WRITING POEMS

This morning I watched
the pale green cones of the rhododendrons
opening their small pink and red blouses—

the bodies of the flowers
were instantly beautiful to the bees, they hurried
out of that dark place in the thick tree

one after another, an invisible line
upon which their iridescence caught fire
as the sun caught them, sliding down.

Is there anything more important
than hunger and happiness? Each bee entered
the frills of a flower to find

the sticky fountain, and if some dust
spilled on the walkways of the petals
and caught onto their bodies, I don't know

if the bees know that otherwise death
is everywhere, even in the red swamp
of a flower. But they did this

with no small amount of desperation—you might say: love.

And the flowers, as daft as mud, poured out their honey.

SOME HERONS

A blue preacher
flew toward the swamp,
in slow motion.

On the leafy banks,
an old Chinese poet,
hunched in the white gown of his wings,

was waiting.
The water
was the kind of dark silk

that has silver lines
shot through it
when it is touched by the wind

or is splashed upward,
in a small, quick flower,
by the life beneath it.

The preacher
made his difficult landing,
his skirts up around his knees.

The poet's eyes
flared, just as a poet's eyes
are said to do

when the poet is awakened
from the forest of meditation.
It was summer.

It was only a few moments past the sun's rising,
which meant that the whole long sweet day
lay before them.

They greeted each other,
rumpling their gowns for an instant,
and then smoothing them.

They entered the water,
and instantly two more herons—
equally as beautiful—

joined them and stood just beneath them
in the black, polished water
where they fished, all day.

FIVE A.M. IN THE PINEWOODS

I'd seen
their hoofprints in the deep
needles and knew
they ended the long night

under the pines, walking
like two mute
and beautiful women toward
the deeper woods, so I

got up in the dark and
went there. They came
slowly down the hill
and looked at me sitting under

the blue trees, shyly
they stepped
closer and stared
from under their thick lashes and even

nibbled some damp
tassels of weeds. This
is not a poem about a dream,
though it could be.

This is a poem about the world
that is ours, or could be.
Finally
one of them—I swear it!—

32

would have come to my arms.
But the other
stamped sharp hoof in the
pine needles like

the tap of sanity,
and they went off together through
the trees. When I woke
I was alone,

I was thinking:
so this is how you swim inward,
so this is how you flow outward,
so this is how you pray.

LITTLE OWL WHO LIVES IN THE ORCHARD

His beak could open a bottle,
and his eyes—when he lifts their soft lids—
go on reading something
just beyond your shoulder—
Blake, maybe,
or the Book of Revelation.

Never mind that he eats only
the black-smocked crickets,
and dragonflies if they happen
to be out late over the ponds, and of course
the occasional festal mouse.
Never mind that he is only a memo
from the offices of fear—

it's not size but surge that tells us
when we're in touch with something real,
and when I hear him in the orchard
fluttering
down the little aluminum
ladder of his scream—
when I see his wings open, like two black ferns,

a flurry of palpitations
as cold as sleet
rackets across the marshlands
of my heart,
like a wild spring day.

Somewhere in the universe,
in the gallery of important things,
the babyish owl, ruffled and rakish,
sits on its pedestal.
Dear, dark dapple of plush!
A message, reads the label,
from that mysterious conglomerate:
Oblivion and Co.
The hooked head stares
from its blouse of dark, feathery lace.
It could be a valentine.

THE GIFT

I wanted to thank the mockingbird for the vigor of his song.
Every day he sang from the rim of the field, while I picked
    blueberries or just idled in the sun.
Every day he came fluttering by to show me, and why not,
    the white blossoms in his wings.
So one day I went there with a machine, and played some songs of
    Mahler.
The mockingbird stopped singing, he came close and seemed
    to listen.
Now when I go down to the field, a little Mahler spills
    through the sputters of his song.
How happy I am, lounging in the light, listening as the music
    floats by!
And I give thanks also for my mind, that thought of giving
    a gift.
And mostly I'm grateful that I take this world so seriously.

PIPEFISH

In the green
  and purple weeds
    called *Zostera*, loosely
      swinging in the shallows,

I waded, I reached
  my hands
    in that most human
      of gestures—to find,

to see,
  to hold whatever it is
    that's there—
      and what came up

wasn't much
  but it glittered
    and struggled,
      it had eyes, and a body

like a wand,
  it had pouting lips.
    No longer,
      all of it,

than any of my fingers,
  it wanted
    away from my strangeness,
      it wanted

to go back
  into that waving forest
    so quick and wet.
      I forget

when this happened,
  how many years ago
    I opened my hands—
      like a promise

I would keep my whole life,
  and have—
    and let it go.
      I tell you this

in case you have yet to wade
  into the green
    and purple shallows
      where the diminutive

pipefish
  wants to go on living.
    I tell you this
      against everything you are—

your human heart,
  your hands passing over the world,
    gathering and closing,
      so dry and slow.

THE KOOKABURRAS

In every heart there is a coward and a procrastinator.
In every heart there is a god of flowers, just waiting
to come out of its cloud and lift its wings.
The kookaburras, kingfishers, pressed against the edge of
their cage, they asked me to open the door.
Years later I wake in the night and remember how I said to them,
no, and walked away.
They had the brown eyes of soft-hearted dogs.
They didn't want to do anything so extraordinary, only to fly
home to their river.
By now I suppose the great darkness has covered them.
As for myself, I am not yet a god of even the palest flowers.
Nothing else has changed either.
Someone tosses their white bones to the dung-heap.
The sun shines on the latch of their cage.
I lie in the dark, my heart pounding.

The Lilies Break Open Over the Dark Water

Inside
   that mud-hive, that gas-sponge,
     that reeking
       leaf-yard, that rippling

dream-bowl, the leeches'
   flecked and swirling
     broth of life, as rich
      as Babylon,

the fists crack
   open and the wands
     of the lilies
       quicken, they rise

like pale poles
   with their wrapped beaks of lace;
     one day
       they tear the surface,

the next they break open
   over the dark water.
     And there you are
      on the shore,

fitful and thoughtful, trying
   to attach them to an idea—
     some news of your own life.
      But the lilies

are slippery and wild—they are
  devoid of meaning, they are
    simply doing,
        from the deepest

spurs of their being,
    what they are impelled to do
      every summer.
          And so, dear sorrow, are you.

Death at a Great Distance

The ripe, floating caps
  of the fly amanita
    glow in the pinewoods.
      I don't even think
        of the eventual corruption of my body,

but of how quaint and humorous they are,
  like a collection of doorknobs,
    half-moons,
      then a yellow drizzle of flying saucers.
      In any case

they won't hurt me unless
  I take them between my lips
    and swallow, which I know enough
      not to do. Once, in the south,
        I had this happen:

the soft rope of a watermoccasin
  slid down the red knees
    of a mangrove, the hundreds of ribs
      housed in their smooth, white
        sleeves of muscle moving it

like a happiness
  toward the water, where some bubbles
    on the surface of that underworld announced
      a fatal carelessness. I didn't
        even then move toward the fine point

of the story, but stood in my lonely body
   amazed and full of attention as it fell
      like a stream of glowing syrup into
         the dark water, as death
            blurted out of that perfectly arranged mouth.

The Notebook

"Six a.m.—
the small, pond turtle
lifts its head
into the air
like a green toe.
It looks around.
What it sees
is the whole world
swirling back from darkness:
a red sun
rising over the water,
over the pines,
and the wind lifting,
and the water-striders heading out,
and the white lilies
opening their happy bodies.
The turtle
doesn't have a word for any of it—
the silky water
or the enormous blue morning,
or the curious affair of his own body.
On the shore
I'm so busy
scribbling and crossing out
I almost miss seeing him
paddle away
through the wet, black forest.
More and more the moments come to me:
how much can the right word do?
Now a few of the lilies

are a faint flamingo inside
their white hearts,
and there is still time
to let the last roses of the sunrise
float down
into my uplifted eyes."

PRAISE

Knee-deep
  in the ferns
    springing up
      at the edge of the whistling swamp,

I watch the owl
  with its satisfied,
    heart-shaped face
      as it flies over the water—

back and forth—
  as it flutters down
    like a hellish moth
      wherever the reeds twitch—

whenever, in the muddy cover,
  some little life sighs
    before it slides into the moonlight
      and becomes a shadow.

In the distance,
  awful and infallible,
    the old swamp belches.
      Of course

it stabs my heart
  whenever something cries out
    like a teardrop.
      But isn't it wonderful,

what is happening
   in the branches of the pines:
      the owl's young,
         dressed in snowflakes,

are starting to fatten—
   they beat their muscular wings,
      they dream of flying
         for another million years

over the water,
   over the ferns,
      over the world's roughage
         as it bleeds and deepens.

LOOKING FOR SNAKES

Because it is good
    to be afraid—
        but not too afraid—
            I walk carefully

up the slabby hill,
    through laces of bracken,
        through the thick, wild roses,
            waiting for my heart

to fly up
    out of the leaves
        chilled
            and singing,

and it does.
    They're there—
        two of them,
            in sleepy loops—

and they rise
    in a spit of energy,
        like dark stalks.
            among the wild, pink roses,

their mouths
    narrow and stubborn,
        their red eyes
            staring.

Do you shiver
    at the mere mention
        of their glossy,
            shoulderless bodies?

I would like to bring you here.
    I would like you to remember
        the black flowers of their faces
            as well as their quick slithering—

I would like you to remember
    the pretty fire that dabs out of their mouths
        as well as the plunge back into the shadows,
            and the heart's thudding song.

FISH BONES

Maybe Michelangelo
   or Picasso
      could have imagined
         these dream shapes,

these curves and thongs,
   snow-needles,
      jaws, brain-cases,
         eye sockets—

somebody, anyway,
   whose mind
      was in some clear kind
         of rapture

and probably
   in the early morning
      when the sun
         on its invisible muscle

was rising
   over the water.
      I don't think
         it was just a floundering

in the darkness,
   no matter
      how much time there was.
         This morning

I picked up something
   like a honey-combed heart,
      and something else
         like a frozen flower

at the foot of the waves
   and I thought of da Vinci—
      the way he kept dreaming
         of what was inside the darkness—

how it wanted to rise
   on its invisible muscle,
      how it wanted to shine
         like fire.

The Oak Tree at the Entrance
to Blackwater Pond

Every day
on my way to the pond
I pass the lightning-felled,
chesty,
hundred-fingered, black oak
which, summers ago,
swam forward when the storm

laid one lean yellow wand against it, smoking it open
to its rosy heart.
It dropped down
in a veil of rain,
in a cloud of sap and fire,
and became what it has been ever since—
a black boat
floating
in the tossing leaves of summer,

like the coffin of Osiris
descending
upon the cloudy Nile.
But, listen, I'm tired of that brazen promise:
death and resurrection.
I'm tired of hearing how the nitrogens will return
to the earth again,
through the hinterland of patience—
how the mushrooms and the yeasts
will arrive in the wind—
how they'll anchor the pearls of their bodies and begin

to gnaw through the darkness,
like wolves at bones—

what I loved, I mean, was *that* tree—
tree of the moment—tree of my own sad, mortal heart—
and I don't want to sing anymore of the way

Osiris came home at last, on a clean
and powerful ship, over
the dangerous sea, as a tall
and beautiful stranger.

EVERYTHING

No doubt in Holland,
when van Gogh was a boy,
there were swans drifting
over the green sea
of the meadows, and no doubt
on some warm afternoon
he lay down and watched them,
and almost thought: this is everything.
What drove him
to get up and look further
is what saves this world,
even as it breaks
the hearts of men.
In the mines where he preached,
where he studied tenderness,
there were only men, all of them
streaked with dust.
For years he would reach
toward the darkness.
But no doubt, like all of us,
he finally remembered
everything, including the white birds,
weightless and unaccountable,
floating around the towns
of grit and hopelessness—
and this is what would finish him:
not the gloom, which was only terrible,
but those last yellow fields, where clearly
nothing in the world mattered, or ever would,
but the insensible light.

NATURE

All night
   in and out the slippery shadows
      the owl hunted,
         the beads of blood

scarcely dry on the hooked beak before
   hunger again seized him
      and he fell, snipping
         the life from some plush breather,

and floated away
   into the crooked branches
      of the trees, that all night
         went on lapping

the sunken rain, and growing,
   bristling life
      spreading through all their branches
         as one by one

they tossed the white moon upward
   on its slow way
      to another morning
         in which nothing new

would ever happen,
   which is the true gift of nature,
      which is the reason
         we love it.

Forgive me.
   For hours I had tried to sleep
    and failed;
      restless and wild,

I could settle on nothing
   and fell, in envy
     of the things of darkness
      following their sleepy course—

the root and branch, the bloodied beak—
   even the screams from the cold leaves
    were as red songs that rose and fell
     in their accustomed place.

SNAKE

And here is the serpent again,
dragging himself out from his nest of darkness,
his cave under the black rocks,
his winter-death.
He slides over the pine needles.
He loops around the bunches of rising grass,
looking for the sun.

Well, who doesn't want the sun after the long winter?
I step aside,
he feels the air with his soft tongue,
around the bones of his body he moves like oil,

downhill he goes
toward the black mirrors of the pond.
Last night it was still so cold
I woke and went out to stand in the yard,
and there was no moon.

So I just stood there, inside the jaw of nothing.
An owl cried in the distance,
I thought of Jesus, how he
crouched in the dark for two nights,
then floated back above the horizon.

There are so many stories,
more beautiful than answers.
I follow the snake down to the pond,

thick and musky he is
as circular as hope.

THE PONDS

Every year
the lilies
are so perfect
I can hardly believe

their lapped light crowding
the black,
mid-summer ponds.
Nobody could count all of them—

the muskrats swimming
among the pads and the grasses
can reach out
their muscular arms and touch

only so many, they are that
rife and wild.
But what in this world
is perfect?

I bend closer and see
how this one is clearly lopsided—
and that one wears an orange blight—
and this one is a glossy cheek

half nibbled away—
and that one is a slumped purse
full of its own
unstoppable decay.

Still, what I want in my life
is to be willing
to be dazzled—
to cast aside the weight of facts

and maybe even
to float a little
above this difficult world.
I want to believe I am looking

into the white fire of a great mystery.
I want to believe that the imperfections are nothing—
that the light is everything—that it is more than the sum
of each flawed blossom rising and fading. And I do.

The Summer Day

Who made the world?
Who made the swan, and the black bear?
Who made the grasshopper?
This grasshopper, I mean—
the one who has flung herself out of the grass,
the one who is eating sugar out of my hand,
who is moving her jaws back and forth instead of up and down—
who is gazing around with her enormous and complicated eyes.
Now she lifts her pale forearms and thoroughly washes her face.
Now she snaps her wings open, and floats away.
I don't know exactly what a prayer is.
I do know how to pay attention, how to fall down
into the grass, how to kneel down in the grass,
how to be idle and blessed, how to stroll through the fields,
which is what I have been doing all day.
Tell me, what else should I have done?
Doesn't everything die at last, and too soon?
Tell me, what is it you plan to do
with your one wild and precious life?

SERENGETI

When he comes,
walking under the baobab,
awash with the sun, or flecked
with patches of shadows—

his curled lip, under the long hair
as rough as a crib of hay,
dappled with black flies—
when he comes,

at night, floating along the edges
of the waterholes—
when he snuffles the ground, and opens
the wet tunnel of his throat, and roars—

I think of the heavy-browed, crouched fishermen
how they stood at dusk
at the rim of the cave and listened
until it came to them

for the first time
the terror and the awe
of the swinging, golden foot
that waits in the darkness.

Can anyone doubt that the lion of Serengeti
is part of the idea of God?
Can anyone doubt that, for those first, almost-upright bodies
in the shadow of Kilimanjaro,

in the lush garden of Africa,
in the continuation of everything beyond each individual thing,
the lion
was both the flower of life and the winch of death—

the bone-breaker,
and the agent of transformation?
No doubt, in the beginning,
he rose out of the grass

like a fire—
as now he rises out of the grass,
like a fire,
gleaming and unapproachable,

and notices me,
and fixes me with his large,
almost fatherly eyes,
and flexes his shoulders.

I don't know
anything so beautiful as the sunlight
in his rough hair.
I don't know

where I have seen such power before—
except perhaps in the chapel
where Michelangelo's God,
tawny and muscular,

tears the land from the firmament
and places the sun in the sky
so that we may live
on the earth,

among the amazements,
and the lion
runs softly through the dust,
and his eyes, under the thick, animal lashes,

are almost tender,
and I don't know when I have been
so frightened,
or so happy.

THE TERNS

The birds shrug off
the slant air,
they plunge into the sea
and vanish
under the glassy edges
of the water,
and then come back,
flying out of the waves,
as white as snow,
shaking themselves,
shaking the little silver fish,
crying out
in their own language,
voices like rough bells—
it's wonderful
and it happens whenever
the tide starts its gushing
journey back, every morning
or afternoon.
This is a poem
about death,
about the heart blanching
in its fold of shadows
because it knows
someday it will be
the fish and the wave
and no longer itself—
it will be those white wings,
flying in and out

of the darkness
but not knowing it—
this is a poem about loving
the world and everything in it:
the self, the perpetual muscle,
the passage in and out, the bristling
swing of the sea.

ROSES, LATE SUMMER

What happens
to the leaves after
they turn red and golden and fall
away? What happens

to the singing birds
when they can't sing
any longer? What happens
to their quick wings?

Do you think there is any
personal heaven
for any of us?
Do you think anyone,

the other side of that darkness,
will call to us, meaning us?
Beyond the trees
the foxes keep teaching their children

to live in the valley.
so they never seem to vanish, they are always there
in the blossom of light
that stands up every morning

in the dark sky.
And over one more set of hills,
along the sea,
the last roses have opened their factories of sweetness

and are giving it back to the world.
If I had another life
I would want to spend it all on some
unstinting happiness.

I would be a fox, or a tree
full of waving branches.
I wouldn't mind being a rose
in a field full of roses.

Fear has not yet occurred to them, nor ambition.
Reason they have not yet thought of.
Neither do they ask how long they must be roses, and then what.
Or any other foolish question.

HERONS IN WINTER IN THE FROZEN MARSH

All winter
two blue herons
hunkered in the frozen marsh,
like two columns of blue smoke.

What they ate
I can't imagine,
unless it was the small laces
of snow that settled

in the ruckus of the cattails,
or the glazed windows of ice
under the tired
pitchforks of their feet—

so the answer is
they ate nothing,
and nothing good could come of that.
They were mired in nature, and starving.

Still, every morning
they shrugged the rime from their shoulders,
and all day they
stood to attention

in the stubbled desolation.
I was filled with admiration,
sympathy,
and, of course, empathy.

It called for a miracle.
Finally the marsh softened,
and their wings cranked open
revealing the old blue light,

so that I thought: how could this possibly be
the blunt, dark finish?
First one, then the other, vanished
into the ditches and upheavals.

All spring, I watched the rising blue-green grass,
above its gleaming and substantial shadows,
toss in the breeze,
like wings.

Looking at a Book of van Gogh's Paintings, in Lewisburg, Pennsylvania

Don't try
    to tell me
        what can or can't
            be done. The snow

is falling again,
    perfectly at leisure
        over the gray,
            thin-haired backs

of the mountains of Pennsylvania.
    I'm far from home.
        And neither are these trees—
            olives and almonds—

home; neither is this
    gathering
        of sunflowers,
            this yellow house,

home. Don't try to tell me
    what one poor
        and lonely Dutchman
            can or can't do

with a brush
    and a roll of canvas
        and his crazy old heart.
            Outside,

the snow floats down,
    it sifts through the crooked branches,
      it doesn't hesitate,
        it settles over the ground

like the white fire
    it was in the beginning,
      wherever it began
        to pour through the black sky—

what a light it becomes
    anywhere at all
      it rubs against this earth—
        this crazy old home.

FOXES IN WINTER

Every night in the moonlight the foxes come down the hill
to gnaw on the bones of birds. I never said
nature wasn't cruel. Once, in a city as hot as these woods
are cold, I met a boy with a broken face. To stay
alive, he was a beggar. Also, in the night, a thief.
And there are birds in his country that look like rainbows—
if he could have caught them, he would have
torn off their feathers and put their bodies into
his own. The foxes are hungry, who could blame them
for what they do? I never said
we weren't sunk in glittering nature, until we are able
to become something else. As for the boy, it's simple.
He had nothing, not even a bird. All night the pines
are so cold their branches crack. All night the snow falls
softly down. Then it shines like a field
of white flowers. Then it tightens.

How Turtles Come to Spend the Winter in the Aquarium, Then Are Flown South and Released Back Into the Sea

Somewhere down beach, in the morning, at water's edge, I found
    a sea turtle,
its huge head a smoldering apricot, its shell streaming with
    seaweed,
its eyes closed, its flippers motionless.
When I bent down, it moved a little.
When I picked it up, it sighed.
Was it forty pounds, or fifty pounds, or a hundred?
Was it two miles back to the car?
We walked a little while, and then we rested, and then we
    walked on.
I walked with my mouth open, my heart roared.
The eyes opened, I don't know what they thought.
Sometimes the flippers swam at the air.
Sometimes the eyes closed.
I couldn't walk anymore, and then I walked some more
while it turned into granite, or cement, but with that
    apricot-colored head,
that stillness, that Buddha-like patience, that cold-shocked
    but slowly beating heart.
Finally, we reached the car.

The afternoon is the other part of this story.
Have you ever found something beautiful, and maybe just in time?
How such a challenge can fill you!

Jesus could walk over the water.
I had to walk ankle-deep in the sand, and I did it.
My bones didn't quite snap.

Come on in, and see me smile.
I probably won't stop for hours.
Already, in the warmth, the turtle has raised its head, is
    looking around.
Today, who could deny it, I am an important person.

CROWS

It is January, and there are the crows
like black flowers on the snow.
While I watch they rise and float toward the frozen pond,
    they have seen
some streak of death on the dark ice.
They gather around it and consume everything, the strings
and the red music of that nameless body. Then they shout,
one hungry, blunt voice echoing another.
It begins to rain.
Later, it becomes February,
and even later, spring
returns, a chorus of thousands.
They bow, and begin their important music.
I recognize the oriole.
I recognize the thrush, and the mockingbird.
I recognize the business of summer, which is to forge ahead,
    delicately.
So I dip my fingers among the green stems, delicately.
I lounge at the edge of the leafing pond, delicately.
I scarcely remember the crust of the snow.
I scarcely remember the icy dawns and the sun like a lamp
    without a fuse.
I don't remember the fury of loneliness.
I never felt the wind's drift.
I never heard of the struggle between anything and nothing.
I never saw the flapping, blood-gulping crows.

MAYBE

Sweet Jesus, talking
   his melancholy madness,
      stood up in the boat
         and the sea lay down,

silky and sorry.
   So everybody was saved
      that night.
         But you know how it is

when something
   different crosses
      the threshold—the uncles
         mutter together,

the women walk away,
   the young brother begins
      to sharpen his knife.
         Nobody knows what the soul is.

It comes and goes
   like the wind over the water—
      sometimes, for days,
         you don't think of it.

Maybe, after the sermon,
   after the multitude was fed,
      one or two of them felt
         the soul slip forth

like a tremor of pure sunlight,
  before exhaustion,
    that wants to swallow everything,
      gripped their bones and left them

miserable and sleepy,
  as they are now, forgetting
    how the wind tore at the sails
      before he rose and talked to it—

tender and luminous and demanding
  as he always was—
    a thousand times more frightening
      than the killer sea.

FINCHES

Ice in the woods, snow in the fields, a few finches singing.
I look up in time to see their raspberry-colored faces
and the black tears on their breasts.
Of course, they are just trying to stay alive
like the frozen river and the crows.
But who would guess that, the way they dangle the bright
necklaces of their music
from the tops of the trees?
Before nightfall, they'd better find where the last sprays of seeds
have fallen,
they'd better find shelter from the wind.
And there they go, tiny rosettes of energy,
as though nothing in this world was frightening—
as though the only thing that mattered was to praise the world
sufficiently—
as though they were only looking, light-heartedly, for the next
tree in which to sing;
and here I am, at home again, out of the snowy fields, where I will
take off my jacket, and sit down at the table, and go over
my verses again.

WHITE OWL FLIES INTO AND OUT OF THE FIELD

Coming down
out of the freezing sky
with its depths of light,
like an angel,
or a buddha with wings,
it was beautiful
and accurate,
striking the snow and whatever was there
with a force that left the imprint
of the tips of its wings—
five feet apart—and the grabbing
thrust of its feet,
and the indentation of what had been running
through the white valleys
of the snow—

and then it rose, gracefully,
and flew back to the frozen marshes,
to lurk there,
like a little lighthouse,
in the blue shadows—
so I thought:
maybe death
isn't darkness, after all,
but so much light
wrapping itself around us—

as soft as feathers—
that we are instantly weary
of looking, and looking, and shut our eyes,

not without amazement,
and let ourselves be carried,
as through the translucence of mica,
to the river
that is without the least dapple or shadow—
that is nothing but light—scalding, aortal light—
in which we are washed and washed
out of our bones.